KT-408-764

GREENHOUSE
GARDENING

RONALD MENAGE

HarperCollins*Publishers*

Products mentioned in this book

ICI Antkiller Dust	contains	pirimiphos-methyl
Benlate* + 'Activex'	contains	benomyl
'Clean-Up'	contains	tar acids
'Fumite' General Purpose Insecticide Smoke	contains	pirimiphos-methyl
'Fumite' Whitefly Smoke	contains	gamma HCH + tecnazine
'Keriguards'	contains	dimethoate
'Keriroot'	contains	NAA + captan
'Kerispray'	contains	pirimiphos-methyl
'Picket'	contains	permethrin
'Rapid'	contains	pirimicarb
'Sybol'	contains	pirimiphos-methyl
ICI Slug Pellets	contains	metaldehyde

Products marked thus *'Sybol'* are trade marks of Imperial Chemical Industries plc
Benlate * is a registered trade mark of Du Pont's
Read the label before you buy: use pesticides safely.

Editors Maggie Daykin, Susanne Mitchell
Designer Chris Walker
Picture research Moira McIlroy

First published 1988 by
HarperCollins Publishers

This edition published 1992
Reprinted 1993

© Marshall Cavendish Limited 1988, 1992

A CIP catalogue record for this book is available from the British Library.

Photoset by Bookworm Typesetting
Printed and bound in Hong Kong by Dai Nippon Printing Company

Front and back cover: Both photographs by The Harry Smith Horticultural
Photographic Collection

CONTENTS

INTRODUCTION

A greenhouse beckons you to enter a world of gardening enchantment and greatly extends the range of plants you can grow, and the period over which they can be enjoyed – including winter. It does more than give aesthetic pleasure – it can also be a sound investment.

Many people find the produce they raise soon pays for the cost of the structure and its maintenance. You can grow your own pot plants, bedding plants, cut flowers, house plants, and a selection of fruits and vegetables for use the year round and the latter will be really fresh and full of flavour.

In a slightly heated greenhouse a wide range of colourful pot plants can be grown. Here is a magnificent but easily achievable display of regal pelargoniums, begonias, salpiglossis and trailing fuchsias. The plant in the hanging basket is one of the small-flowered calceolarias.

Greenhouse gardening can quickly become a fascinating hobby – just the pastime to relieve the stress of everyday life or add enjoyment to retirement. Many infirm or disabled people can manage a greenhouse well, and benefit from the protection it affords them from adverse weather. Older children can derive much fun from growing plants under glass, and some schools and rehabilitation centres have found greenhouse work an invaluable form of education.

Unheated greenhouses Many hardy plants are grown to advantage in a greenhouse without any artificial heat. The sun's warmth it traps keeps the temperature above that outdoors, even in winter. Hardy plants that would be damaged by severe frost, snow, damp atmosphere, heavy rains, hail and wind, will thrive. Examples are alpine plants, hardy and some half-hardy annuals, small shrubs such as young camellias in pots, and many plants usually seen growing outdoors only in sheltered parts of the South and West of the country. Or you could grow crops like winter lettuces and hardy flowers for cutting like *Helleborus niger* (Christmas Rose), as well as a host of hardy bulbs, and the long-stemmed polyanthus.

Heated greenhouses By providing just enough artificial heat to keep the greenhouse frost free in winter, your scope for growing the more tender plants is greatly increased. You can also be sure to save fuchsias, geraniums and the like over winter. With a higher winter minimum of about 5–7°C (41–45°F) the range is enormous and you can grow plants from all of the temperate regions of the world and a fair selection of exotics.

Higher temperatures than this can prove expensive to maintain and anyway are undesirable, if not harmful, for most of our favourite plants. Very warm greenhouses are only for those who specialize in sub-tropical and tropical plants. Extra heat can be provided whenever it is required, by using a propagator or frame, or a small home-made case, fitted with electric soil-warming cables or even warmed by a small paraffin heater.

Conservatories This form of greenhouse gardening is a delightful way to grow plants to form an attractive year-round display. Extra colour and interest are provided by adding groups of seasonal flowering plants as they become decorative. The ideal conservatory is a lean-to that can be entered from your home. It can be heated or unheated as you prefer provided that suitable plants are selected. Modern conservatories are usually modest compared with the grand Victorian structures, yet still extremely pleasing to the eye.

LEFT Colour in a conservatory can be provided by groups of seasonal plants, like these schizanthus which flower in spring or summer.

BELOW LEFT Cold frames can be used in the summer for growing low tender crops like these sweet peppers or capsicums.

Frames These are very useful for supplementing the greenhouse. They can be used to grow many plants that need little height, saving valuable greenhouse space. Outdoors they can be used for hardening off bedding plants, and for growing, propagating, and resting hardy plants. Inside they can be heated and used to germinate seeds, root cuttings, or start plants into growth.

CHOOSING A GREENHOUSE

Greenhouses now come in many shapes and sizes and a choice of materials. Do decide what you want to grow *before* you buy one, so you can choose the design that suits your purpose exactly. Study catalogues from several well-known firms and try to examine the preferred buildings at a garden centre before making your decision.

Size The most popular size is 3 × 2.4m (10 × 8ft) but you could buy a much smaller one if necessary. Buy the biggest you can afford and accommodate on the site, as you can soon fill a greenhouse. Some structures can be extended by adding extra sections later. But if you intend heating your greenhouse, limit its size according to the heating costs you can afford.

Shape A square or rectangular shape makes best use of space, though some people prefer a round greenhouse as it can make a very attractive garden feature.

The barn or span-roof type is the most popular. Some have sloped sides (the Dutch light shape) which provide extra stability in a windy garden and higher light entry.

Lean-to greenhouses are usually the cheapest to heat and if facing south trap much free solar warmth. Some lean-to models also have a sloping side.

Most designs can have dwarf base walls of timber, brick or prefabricated sheeting, which reduce heat loss. But they can also limit the light and therefore the space for growing things. Some designs have the south side glazed to the ground, some have a base wall and others have base panels that can be fitted in winter and removed in summer. But the total glass-to-ground house is the most versatile.

There must be enough ventilators. A greenhouse up to 2.4 × 3m (8 × 10ft) should have at least two – one side vent and one top vent. Larger sizes must have more. You don't have to use them all at once, but selectively according to the wind direction.

Many structures now have built-in gutters – valuable because rainwater can otherwise undermine the foundations and seep in, making the inside damp and cold. Don't use water collected from the gutters to water your greenhouse plants (see Hygiene, page 26).

Framework Aluminium alloy is rapidly taking the place of timber for home greenhouses. It does not deteriorate like timber, needs negligible maintenance and should last a lifetime. Some alloy greenhouses now have an attractive white, green or bronze finish. Being lightweight, alloy frames can be sold as kits and are easily carried home from a garden centre in a car.

Some people still prefer timber. Red cedar is popular for its handsome appearance and long life. All timbers should be treated against rotting, preferably before you buy them. Regular renovation or painting is essential too.

When choosing, look for a strong ridge bar. A wooden ridge bar may sag after a time, so the sides bulge and the glass doesn't fit properly.

Glass or plastic? Glass glazing is best for maximum heat retention, trapping solar warmth and ensuring a long-lived structure. But plastics are valuable alternatives where there is a high risk of breakage. UVI grade polythene has a longer life when exposed to sunlight so it is very useful for portable structures.

LEFT A span-roof greenhouse in western red cedar, a long-lasting and attractive wood.

RIGHT Lean-to greenhouses are cheaper to heat than free-standing ones. Those with glass virtually to ground level are the most versatile. Most have an aluminium framework but timber-framed lean-tos are available if preferred.

RIGHT A round greenhouse makes an attractive garden feature and models in aluminium or timber are available. Such a house is ideal for a small garden but bear in mind that it can heat up rapidly in summer so careful attention must be paid to ventilation.

SITING AND ERECTING

Before you put up a greenhouse, consult your local authority, landlord and neighbours, as legal and planning requirements may have to be satisfied. One attached to a dwelling may be rateable, though the charge will be small. There should be no problems with a small free-standing house.

Site Greenhouses can be sited almost anywhere – even on a roof or balcony. But the site will affect the greenhouse environment and what will thrive inside it. An open position that gets plenty of winter light and free warmth from the sun is best. It's easy to shade it when necessary. A greenhouse *can* be sited in the shade, but you could then grow only shade-loving plants.

Keep it away from large trees, especially evergreens, but do site it near your home to make it cheaper and easier to provide electricity, gas or water. Never erect one on ground that's waterlogged or very damp in winter or it will become cold and humid, which plants hate. Also avoid places where frost collects. Try to protect an exposed greenhouse with a nearby wall, fence or hedge but without shading it too much.

ABOVE Plants can be grown against a greenhouse if it has side walls.

BELOW Staging for pot plants is usually available from greenhouse makers.

Orientation To get full benefit from the low winter sun, range a rectangular greenhouse east-west. It is then enough to shade its south side in summer. The way a lean-to faces has a dramatic effect on its use. A north-facing house is shaded, except in early morning and late in the day. Most popular plants thrive in the cool shade in summer, but it can be very chilly in winter.

A south-facing lean-to can become far too hot in summer and needs heavy shading, but in winter it can be delightfully warm on bright days. A lean-to facing west can hold afternoon and evening warmth to keep it warmer overnight than one facing east. Always choose plants to suit your conditions.

Erecting Manufacturers supply full instructions and a small greenhouse can usually be erected in a few hours with a few tools, often single-handed. Foundation plinths offered as extras are generally well worth having. Erect the greenhouse on firm, level ground. Form a simple foundation by digging a shallow trench of the required dimensions and pouring in a fairly fluid cement mix. Some greenhouses are secured by ground anchors instead; these are simple to install if you follow the instructions provided.

Glazing is now usually done with clips and/or plastic strip, though mastic is sometimes used for this purpose. Putty is rarely used.

Fittings Most greenhouses need staging and shelves to display plants. These are usually offered as extras by the greenhouse supplier. You may prefer to leave the brighter south side clear for taller plants like tomatoes.

A maximum and minimum thermometer is essential for recording

TOP A rectangular greenhouse should be ranged east to west.

ABOVE Shelves can be used for displaying plants, and for seedlings.

temperatures while you are away. Various automatic ventilation and watering systems are available too – invaluable if you are sometimes away for long periods.

The floor can be levelled and firmed and strewn with clean shingle. It is not advisable to grow plants in the ground within the greenhouse (see Hygiene, page 26).

HEATING

The cost of heating a home greenhouse should be quite modest unless unsuitable equipment is used or heat is not conserved. Never heat a greenhouse to a higher temperature than necessary.

An electricity supply, together with control panel and sockets for electrical appliances such as heaters and propagating cases, should be installed by a qualified electrician and, of course, must be fully water and damp proof.

Heat requirement You can assess how much heat is required in British Thermal Units (or watts for electricity) from the greenhouse's dimensions and the minimum temperature you require. Good heater suppliers will suggest suitable heater ratings given these figures. Don't buy a heater until you know your requirements; neither should you buy one whose rating is unknown.

There is now little difference between the costs of various fuels if you take their efficiency into account. Make sure no draughts can enter your greenhouse or they will cancel out the benefits of a heater.

A small greenhouse can be easily and cheaply insulated by lining with clear polythene sheeting or bubble plastic, which will cut heat loss by 40–50 per cent. Try to trap 13mm–2.5cm (½-1in) of still air between glass and plastic. The plastic can be fixed to timber frames with drawing pins. Special fittings are available for use with metal frames.

Electric heating Electricity is highly efficient when thermostatically controlled and does not contaminate the air with fumes or produce excessive humidity. Electrically heated houses need little ventilation, particularly if fan heaters are used. These keep the air moving, so the plants are remarkably free from moulds and mildews. Some models have heat and fan controls linked, so that both go off together, but others have a continuously running fan. Only use the latter in a well-lined greenhouse or it could speed heat loss through the sides. Convector heaters and heating tubes are also popular. Distribute tubes around the greenhouse, don't bank them all in one place.

12

Gas heating The special natural gas heaters are very effective and thermostatically controlled. Provide some ventilation while the heater is operating, to supply air to the burner and avoid fumes and excessive humidity. Ventilate freely when the heater is off and weather permits.

Paraffin wick heaters Always keep a greenhouse 'lamp' ready as a standby in case other heaters fail, or to provide extra heat in a freak cold spell. They are reliable and portable. Paraffin was once the cheapest fuel, but now costs much the same as other fuels. Ventilate as for gas heaters – this is vital. A blue-flame burner is by far the best, giving maximum efficiency with minimum fumes. Oil lamps will need tending regularly as thermostatic control has not proved very successful.

Use only the best grade domestic paraffin, keep heaters clean and wicks trimmed. The delicate leaves of some plants like young tomatoes can be browned by paraffin fumes.

Hot water pipes These used to be the usual way of heating a greenhouse. Today they are used mainly in larger greenhouses and those that need quite high temperatures. Small boilers are also obtainable for home greenhouses and can usually be operated by solid fuel or oil. Modern equipment is very easy to install and lightweight aluminium alloy pipes are used instead of the old cast iron ones. Modern boilers are also thermostatically controlled.

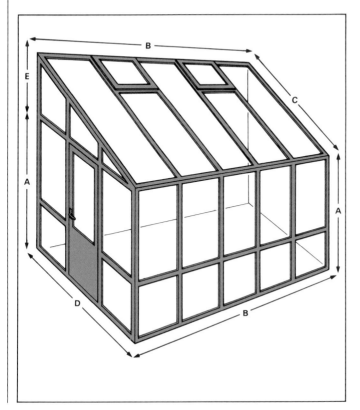

To establish the size of heater required, first measure the greenhouse to calculate the area of glass and floor. You will need all the dimensions shown in the illustration, and you should take these with you when you choose your heater. Also tell the supplier whether you have a lean-to or full-span greenhouse. This information will enable the supplier to advise on the size of heater required.

VENTILATION AND SHADES

Many beginners fail with their greenhouses because they let them get over-heated by not admitting enough air. On a sunny day an unshaded, unventilated house sited in an open place can soon trap sufficient heat to scorch or even kill the plants inside.

Summer ventilation is obviously necessary but winter ventilation is also vital. If the air is cold, humid and stagnant, plants soon fall victim to mildew. (See also Gas and paraffin heating, page 13.)

Ventilation equipment Greenhouse vents are either hinged windows with stay-bars or formed of louvres. Some louvres don't fit snugly and let in draughts. Check your greenhouse does not suffer from this fault. You must have control over all the air that enters it. Side vents are best sited low in the sides to give a better air change. Warm air escaping from open roof vents draws cool air in from below. Open vents according to wind direction and don't let air rush through the house in windy weather or its force could damage plants.

You can fit non-electric thermo-operated vent controllers (sold at most garden centres) for automatic ventilation – or thermostatically-controlled electric extractor fans. Solar-operated fans are available if there is no electricity supply.

Winter ventilation Ventilate freely when the outdoor temperature is higher than the minimum greenhouse temperature you need. But use vents carefully when houses are heated. Excessive use or forgetting to close vents only wastes heat. Line vents separately in houses heated with paraffin or gas without a flue, so they can still be used to remove fumes and condensation.

Louvre ventilators are often fitted in the sides of greenhouses and are used in conjunction with roof vents. Greenhouse vegetables, like these tomatoes and cucumbers, together with most other plants, need good ventilation.

14

Roof ventilators are essential and often it is worth ordering more than are supplied as standard. They can be opened and closed automatically by means of non-electric thermo-operated vent controllers.

Summer ventilation Too much summer ventilation dries out the greenhouse rapidly, though this is no problem where automatic watering is used. To keep down temperatures effectively, ventilate in conjunction with shading and damping down (see Watering, pages 24-25).

Shading Unless in a shady position, most greenhouses need some shading – perhaps on one side – in summer to prevent overheating and scorched plants. Slatted blinds are fine but expensive and need to be custom made. Interior blinds can be made from cheaper materials but are less effective, as the sun's rays should be stopped *before* they get through the glass. But fitting the interior with blinds could prevent damage by scalding or scorching.

Shading paints are cheap and convenient, though some home-made mixes can damage the structure. Coolglass on the other hand adheres to the glass by electrostatic action. This instant-mix shading is easy to apply, fast even in torrential rain, yet can be wiped off easily with a duster. It is brilliant white and cools the greenhouse efficiently. Green used to be thought the correct colour for shading materials, but this is quite wrong. White reflects most light and therefore heat.

In mid-winter plants need maximum light, so keep the glass clean and unobstructed. But be ready to shade early in the year, about late February, when the sun's heat can cause severe wilting particularly in the case of plants such as cinerarias, calceolarias and primulas.

POTTING AND FEEDING

Soil is rarely used for growing pot plants unless it has been sterilized (see Hygiene, page 26), as it is liable to be infested with pests, diseases and weed seeds. The ground inside a greenhouse will be similarly contaminated and is best not used. Most plants grow well in pots, larger ones in growing bags, but use proper seed or potting composts for best results.

LEFT Lettuces and other vegetables can be grown in plastic pots as well as in growing bags.

BELOW Growing bags are large plastic sacks filled with special compost. They are ideal for tomatoes and other vigorous growers.

Composts Proper use of composts, pots, potting and feeding will bring success, slapdash methods only disappointment. Two main types of compost are used – one for seed sowing, the other – such as 'Keri-compost' - for potting, though universal composts are available which suit both jobs. Other useful types are for rooting cuttings and there are lime-free ericaceous composts for acid lovers like heathers. John Innes composts made to the original specifications are excellent, but rarely reach this standard. All these composts are sold ready made.

You can also buy packets of balanced fertilizers to add to your own peat or peat/grit mix. All these composts have the right open texture for plant roots and an ideal balance and amount of essential nutrients.

Pots and bags Plastic pots are easy to clean, and to sterilize if necessary, and plants don't dry out so quickly as in clay pots. ICI flat pack polythene pots are a good choice, especially if you happen to be short of storage space.

Most useful sizes are 7.5cm (3in) and 13cm (5in) but smaller and larger sizes will be needed. Half-pots, half the normal depth, are useful for shallow-rooted plants and many bulbs. Hanging baskets will be needed for trailing plants. Plastic pots can be hung if drilled round the rim and fitted with wires.

Growing bags are large plastic sacks filled with special compost. The bag is laid flat and holes cut for the plants – usually vigorous growers such as tomatoes, cucumbers, melons and aubergines.

Other useful products include disposable fibre pots and peat or biodegradable pots which can be left on the plant to rot down when potting on or planting out. Plastic trays are used for seed sowing and for growing on the young seedlings.

Potting A convenient potting bench can be made for a small greenhouse from a sheet of easily cleaned zinc or aluminium (from a builder's merchant), with two sides and the back turned up to form a large three-sided tray. This can fit on the staging and be stored when not required.

Make sure pots are thoroughly clean before use (see Hygiene, page 26). Never use a larger pot than necessary. Modern pots filled with modern compost do not need the drainage holes covered, but clay pots or others with large holes may need a few pieces of broken pot placed over the holes to stop compost falling through. When potting a plant leave about 19mm ($\frac{3}{4}$in) between the rim and the top of the compost for watering. It helps you assess how much water you are giving too.

Compost should be nicely moist for potting – neither wet nor dust-dry. Do not make it too firm. Just tap the pot firmly on the bench after potting to consolidate the compost. Soak clay pots well overnight before use. They are also easier to scrub clean if well soaked.

Line hanging baskets with moss to improve their appearance, then spread thin polythene, slit for drainage, over it and fill with compost. Special composts for hanging baskets are now widely available.

Peat pots are useful for growing on plants individually. Remove the weaker seedlings.

The pots are planted along with the plants to avoid disturbance of the root system.

Potting on Always use a pot just large enough to take the plant, unless it is very vigorous, then pot on into slightly larger pots as it develops. There is then always some *fresh* compost for the roots to grow into. A plant may need potting on several times before it reaches maturity. Give an extra 2.5cm (1in) of compost round the roots each time. A plant needs attention if there is a mass of roots round its root ball. Tap it out of its pot and give it a larger one, or repot it (see below).

To remove a plant from its pot, first make sure the compost is moist, then invert it, supporting the base of the plant between your fingers. Tap the rim sharply on the bench edge to release the root ball, then remove the pot with your other hand.

Repotting An established plant in its final pot often benefits from re-potting. Remove the plant, reduce the size of the root ball, then pot it in the same size of pot with fresh compost. Do this just before the plant resumes growth.

Feeding Most modern composts such as 'Kericompost' contain enough nutrients to supply the plant for a month to six weeks. They also contain slow-release fertilizers and trace elements. When a plant can no longer be potted on and has reached maturity feeding becomes essential. Vigorous plants also demand plenty of food.

Never use mixtures of your own concoction, which could do more harm than good. Use properly ba-

| This plant is clearly ready for potting on – note the tight mass of compacted roots. | The new pot should allow for an additional 2.5 cm (1 in) of compost around the roots. | The fresh compost should then be lightly or moderately firmed with the fingers. |

LEFT Cyclamen growing in modern plastic and traditional terracotta clay pots.

RIGHT 'Kerispikes' are inserted into the compost where they release foods very gradually over a period of about eight weeks. They are ideal for beginners and those gardeners who tend to overfeed their plants.

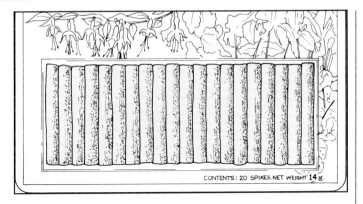

CONTENTS: 20 SPIKES.NET WEIGHT 14 g.

lanced feeds like ICI Liquid Growmore or 'Kerigrow'. These contain all the necessary nutrients in the right proportions. Feed according to the instructions, as over-feeding can be harmful. Little and often is generally the best rule.

'Kerispikes' are ideal for beginners and those who tend to overfeed their plants and they reduce work for busy gardeners. Insert spikes in the compost to release nutrients gradually for about eight weeks.

A plant needs feeding if it is weak, with pale leaves or shoot tips, or its growth is abnormally slow. Many plants need regular feeding as soon as they start to form flower buds. But no plant can absorb food if it is dry, so make sure the compost is moist. Fertilizers given when the compost is dry, particularly if they are not well diluted, could damage plant roots.

PROPAGATION

Beginners will probably start by buying in many plants, rooted cuttings and bulbs, corms and tubers. Most of these can later be propagated from cuttings or division to make more plants cheaply. Do master the technique of raising from seed, as it is economical and exciting. Seedsmen offer new choice varieties each year, with bedding and outdoor plants among them.

Health rules Only propagate from healthy plants that have done well, as faults and diseases can be passed on. Destroy any plants with yellowing or mottled foliage or that are stunted or deformed – signs of virus infection. Buy seeds only from reliable seedsmen.

Propagators Usually, propagating demands higher temperatures than your greenhouse will provide, so you will need a propagator – a small case with a transparent lid to retain warmth and moisture. It is warmed by thermostatically controlled electric cables in the base or with a paraffin heater. Choose a propagator to suit your requirements at a garden centre. Or build your own from a frame with warming cables or a small paraffin heater under it. Spread sand in the bottom and keep it moist to provide humidity and to distribute heat evenly. Basal warmth is known as 'bottom heat'. Aim for temperatures between 15–25°C (60–77°F). Cool climate plants can generally be propagated at the lower end of this range, warm climate ones at the upper end. Warmer temperatures are needed to germinate seeds and root cuttings, after which they can be lowered.

LEFT A large propagator which is heated by means of electric warming cables. It has a built-in thermostat so is economical to run.

RIGHT Many kinds of seeds can be raised in a propagator, after which they are pricked out and given maximum light.

FAR RIGHT Seedlings must be pricked out into seed trays as soon as they are large enough to handle easily.

A propagator should be able to take several seed trays with enough headroom for pots. Do not heat it extravagantly. Most plants need only about 18°C (64°F). Never let it dry out, nor site it in direct sun. A small propagator can be very productive if seed sowing and starting plants into growth are done in planned sequence.

Seed raising Many plants are offered as F1 hybrids. Seeds saved from such plants and others from specially selected parents will not yield identical seedlings, so don't save their seeds. But you could save seeds from species if you wish. Use a proper moist seed compost and sow seeds thinly and evenly in clean plastic seed trays. Cover seeds with a layer of compost as deep as they are thick – fine seeds not at all. Some seeds germinate best in light, others need the dark. Refer to the seed packet or learn from experience. Water in with a fine mist from a sprayer and use it for later watering too. Do not plunge containers to water them.

Never let seeds dry out after sowing or they will not germinate. Stand the seed trays in your propagator or cover them with a sheet of clean white paper, then a piece of glass, or slip the trays into polythene bags and stand them on staging. The paper retains the moisture but stops condensation dripping on to the compost. Overwatering or sowing too deeply will suffocate seeds and stop germination. Most common greenhouse seeds come up in 2-4 weeks.

Some seeds have a hard seed coat and these germinate more quickly if first soaked in water overnight. If they are large enough you can remove a sliver of skin with a razor blade or rub the surface with sandpaper, but do not damage the interior. Typical hard seeds are those of lupins, cannas and sweet peas.

Pricking out Do this as soon as the seedlings are large enough to handle safely. Hold them by their leaves, not the stems. Move into potting compost in pots or seed trays.

Stem cuttings Cuttings are best taken in spring or early autumn. Cut off small vigorous shoots a few inches long, remove lower leaves and cut cleanly across just under a leaf joint. Dip the end about 13mm (½in) deep in 'Keriroot' hormone rooting powder. Insert about 4cm

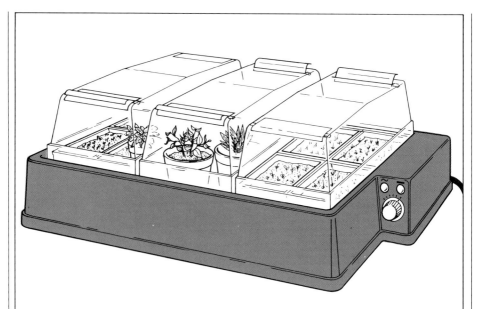

A sophisticated propagator which will hold three full-size seed trays or pots of cuttings. The clear plastic tops have ventilators, as stale air must be avoided with all methods of propagation.

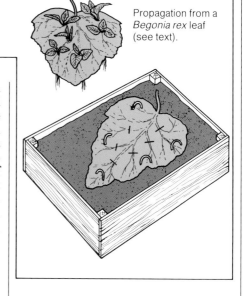

Propagation from a *Begonia rex* leaf (see text).

(1½in) deep in a rooting medium such as 'Kericompost', water in and cover containers with polythene bags to keep moist. Cuttings in a propagator do not need covering but mist them with water regularly so they never dry out. Most cuttings of greenhouse plants are 'soft' and root easily in a couple of weeks in summer or in a warm propagator. When rooted, pot them on individually in suitable compost, firming gently.

Leaf cuttings Some plants – certain begonias, for example – can be grown from healthy mature leaves. Detach a leaf, slit the leaf veins underneath in several places then rest it on compost in a propagator. Roots develop from the wounds and form tiny plants. Pot these separately and grow on. Root sections from the long narrow leaves of streptocarpus or sansevieria like stem cuttings. Saintpaulia (African violet) leaves will root if detached with a piece of leaf stalk and inserted in compost like stem cuttings.

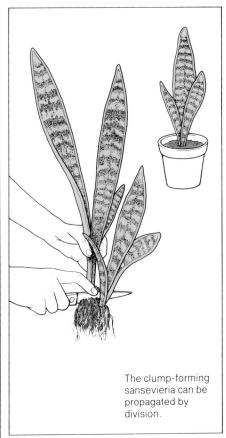

The clump-forming sansevieria can be propagated by division.

can be removed when repotting and grown on. Some tubers and rhizomes reproduce in a similar way. These young bulbs and tubers may take several years to reach flowering size, though some, like gloriosas, flower during their first year.

Layering This method is used for climbers and trailers. Lead a piece of stem into a small pot of rooting compost and bury it just under the surface. Slit the stem at that point or pull away a leaf. Dust the wound with 'Keriroot' to encourage quick rooting. When healthy roots have formed, sever the stem from its parent and pot it separately.

Division This is easy for plants that form well-defined clumps. Cut through the clump and roots with a sharp knife and pot each piece separately, preferably in early spring. Each clump should make several new plants. Remove damaged roots before potting and water, cautiously, until growth begins.

Many tubers and corms form several shoots when started into growth. These can be cut, so that each section has a shoot, and potted separately. Dust cut surfaces with Benlate + 'Activex' or green sulphur to protect from rotting.

Offsets Mature bulbs often form tiny bulblets round their sides which

The chlorophytum or spider plant is propagated by a form of layering. The young plantlets can be pegged down into individual pots, when they will quickly take root. Then sever from parent plant.

WATERING

Pot plants and greenhouse plants must be watered properly if they are to thrive. Those grown in small containers are bound to dry out quickly at times, but don't overwater them. This can be disastrous for the plants – far worse than underwatering.

Roots kept very wet will rot, but underwatered plants usually recover when next watered. Plants with bulbs, tubers, rhizomes, corms or fleshy roots are particularly likely to rot if overwatered. Constant underwatering is wrong too. Even cacti need adequate moisture during their growing season.

When to water Plants cannot use water while dormant or resting, so give them little if any. When the

A capillary watering system consisting of trays and capillary matting, which is kept moist by means of a water reservoir. The plants take up the moisture they need from the matting and, of course, they can be left if you want to go away for a few days or if you tend to be forgetful.

weather is dull and cool, as in winter, plants again need little water. Keep plants on the dry side in very cold weather. During warm bright weather from spring to autumn they need generous watering. As the

24

TOP Some of these geraniums are standing on capillary matting which keeps them moist.

ABOVE A fully automatic greenhouse with watering system and electric heating.

ing to the type of plant, its needs and the light and temperature conditions. A vigorous tomato plant may need watering several times a day in midsummer. Keep the compost nicely moist. A moisture meter could help you.

If the watering space left when potting is filled with water, which is then allowed to soak into the compost, it usually moistens the compost right through. Never stand pots in bowls of water, except in an emergency. Experienced gardeners can detect when a plant needs water because it starts to wilt.

Use only clean water for pot plants or you will lose the benefits gained from sterilized composts. Collect rainwater for acid-loving plants in bowls and store in sealed containers. Avoid rainwater collected from roofs, which is full of pests, diseases and weed seeds.

Equipment Use a can with a long narrow spout which will reach the back of the staging easily. You will also need a sprayer to spray plants when damping down and for watering seeds and seedlings. Automatic aids are also available.

Capillary matting, such as the one made by ICI, is particularly useful for home greenhouses as it provides a very efficient self-watering system for pot plants.

A watering lance attached to a mains hose is the quickest way to water a large greenhouse.

Damping down This simply means wetting the floor and staging during warm weather to reduce water loss from plants by increasing atmospheric humidity. Watering can be done less often. Combined with ventilation, it lowers the temperature, because water absorbs heat from its surroundings as it evaporates.

temperature rises plants lose a lot of water by transpiration through their leaves. Limit this by keeping the air nicely humid by damping down (see below right).

Plants that are cropping, like tomatoes and cucumbers, also need plenty of water. Erratic watering then can result in fruits shrivelling, being shed while immature, or skin splitting – common with tomatoes.

Routine watering is best done in early morning, so your plants start the day well. They cannot use water after dark anyway. Avoid high humidity at night.

How much? You cannot water with exact doses. You must do it accord-

PESTS AND DISEASES

Cleanliness and regular checks for pests and diseases are vitally important in a greenhouse. If prompt action is taken, problems and disappointment can easily be prevented or quickly overcome.

General hygiene
• Don't bring sickly plants into the greenhouse, nor hang on to any that become sick if you cannot cure them. These troubles spread rapidly and put other plants at risk.
• Do not use unsterilized garden soil or crude animal manures, which can cause both disease and weed problems.
• Do not water plants with dirty rainwater, which could introduce pests, diseases, weeds, slimes, mosses and algae.
• Thoroughly clean all pots, trays and other containers. Sterilize them with 'Clean-Up' (see below).
• Inspect all plants daily, or as often as possible, particularly underneath the foliage where many pests and diseases first appear. Act immediately if you find any, to avoid a more serious outbreak.

Sterilizing the greenhouse It is wise to do this each year. The best agent is a phenolic emulsion like 'Clean-Up', which should be used according to the manufacturer's instructions. Diluted as recommended, it can be used to wash down glass, staging and other parts of the structure and sprinkled on to paths and the floor.

Many pests and diseases overwinter in crevices in the structure, usually as spores or tiny eggs. The disinfectant will destroy most of them before they can multiply. Diluted 'Clean-Up' is best applied with a sprayer giving a coarse spray. Don't inhale the mist or get it in your eyes. You could otherwise use a whitewash brush. Remove all plants before disinfection and air the house well for several days before returning them. Let all fumes clear. A slight phenolic smell will linger but does no harm.

The greenhouse soil can also be sterilized with 'Clean-Up', as described on the label. Allow several weeks for fumes to disperse before planting. Even so, don't use the soil year after year. 'Clean-Up' also kills and helps remove slimes, mosses and algae which grow on the glass and floor. In some areas lichens, slimes and mosses can disfigure the exterior and obscure the glass. But don't treat pots or trays containing plants with phenolic emulsion.

PESTS AND DISEASES
Ants Often invade the compost in pots via drainage holes and disturb the plants' roots so they wilt. Puff ICI Antkiller Dust into the drainage holes, under the pots and where the pests are active. The ants should vanish quite quickly.

Ants tunnel under roots, causing wilts.

26

Greenfly on tomato plant.

Botrytis on strawberry.

Aphids Include the familiar greenfly, common in greenhouses and found all year round. An insecticide such as 'Rapid' is a very quick exterminator that can be sprayed on most ornamentals, though not in bright sunlight. Fumigate with 'Fumite' General Purpose Insecticide Smokes where there are vegetables and fruits, particularly cucumbers or melons.

Botrytis (Grey mould) A grey to brown mould that attacks dead and living tissues. Most plants can be affected, lettuces and geraniums severely. Improve hygiene and ventilation and avoid a damp stagnant atmosphere. Fumigate regularly with 'Fumite' Tecnalin Smokes, or spray with Benlate + 'Activex'.

Damping off Seedlings rot at the base and topple over following fungus infection. Reliable composts and good hygiene make it unlikely. If noticed, however, spray all seedlings with Cheshunt Compound (from garden shops) or with Benlate + 'Activex' to check this disease.

LEFT Snails are well-known garden pests.

ABOVE Red spider mite attack can be devastating.

Earwigs Well-known pests active at night, flying from their hiding places in the greenhouse structure. They chew petals and leaves, leaving ragged edges, and also seedlings. Spray with 'Picket', which can be used safely on most crops, including food crops.

Leaf miner A tiny grub that burrows inside leaves, making meandering whitish tunnels, particularly in chrysanthemums and cinerarias. Spray with 'Sybol' or 'Picket'.

Mealy bug Tiny, oval, scale-like insects with grey to white waxy mealy coating which colonize cacti and fleshy-leaved plants. Spray with 'Sybol' or fumigate with 'Fumite' General Purpose Insecticide Smokes. Wipe off small colonies with cotton wool or an artist's brush moistened with methylated spirit.

Red spider mite A pest mainly of the warmer months when humidity is low. Can attack popular plants like carnations, fuchsias, cucumbers and young polyanthus. If foliage appears yellowish or a plant looks sickly inspect under leaves with a strong lens. Minute spider-like mites and tiny whitish spherical eggs show red spider is present. Act immediately as it spreads rapidly with devastating results. Mist plants regularly with clean water during hot weather. Spray with 'Kerispray' or 'Sybol' or use 'Fumite' General Purpose Insecticide Smokes every 7 days until clear.

Scale insects These tiny cream to brownish insects attack succulents and similar plants, in the same way as mealy bugs. A sooty mould can grow on their secretions near the site of attack. Wipe this off and spray with 'Sybol' or 'Kerispray'.

Slugs, snails, woodlice Three well-known garden pests that often invade the greenhouse, doing considerable damage. Sprinkle ICI Slug Pellets around and on pots and seed trays as a preventive. Use ICI Antkiller dust against woodlice.

Sooty mould An unsightly blackish mould that grows on the secretions of aphids, scale insects and white fly. Wipe it off with cotton wool soaked in a weak detergent solution and control the pest responsible.

Thrips These tiny insects cause white patches surrounded by black specks on foliage. Shake plants and the insects will fall out. Spray with 'Sybol', 'Picket' or 'Kerispray'.

Virus diseases Can cause yellowing and mottled foliage, stunting, distortion, and streaking of flowers and leaves. There is no cure, so burn infected plants. Viruses are highly infectious and can be spread by sap-sucking insects and by careless handling.

Whitefly Tiny flies with greyish-white wings that swarm round plants, which are covered with sooty mould. Clear any weeds near the greenhouse, like nettles, which encourage them. Fumigate with 'Fumite' Whitefly Smokes or spray with 'Picket'.

Using Pesticides Read the labels and follow the manufacturer's instructions exactly. Check that the pesticide will not damage your kinds of plant – cucumbers and melons may be susceptible. When fumigating a greenhouse, if there are small children about lock the door until all fumes have cleared.

'Keriguards' provide an easy means of feeding pot plants and protecting them from insect pests at the same time. These long-lasting tablets contain a fertilizer and slow-release systemic insecticide which protects against aphids, mealy bugs and red spider mite.

Mealy bugs in action.

Tomato mosaic.

POPULAR PLANTS

Here are brief descriptions of the most widely grown decorative greenhouse plants. Most need little more than frost-free conditions so they are within the scope of everyone who runs a small greenhouse.

LEFT Achimenes, popularly known as hot-water plants, can be grown in pots or in hanging baskets.

BELOW The giant double-flowered begonias are grown from tubers started into growth early in the year. They flower during the summer.

Bedding plants

The seedsmen offer a host of delightful bedders. Sow between January and early spring. Transplant into seed trays but do not overcrowd them. Grow them on in the greenhouse or a frost-free frame then about two weeks before planting out time (late May to early June) *harden them off* by gradually giving cooler conditions, more light and air in cold frames. Popular bedders like petunias, begonias and *Phlox drummondii* also make good pot plants. Some annuals e.g. Schizanthus, salpiglossis can be sown under glass in autumn and grown on in pots over winter to flower in spring.

Spring-flowering bulbs

Hyacinths, narcissi and tulips make lovely pot plants. Pot between September and November in good potting compost, with the tips of the bulbs just showing, and plunge *outdoors* in moist peat or sand protected from waterlogging. Leave for 6-8 weeks, then bring into the greenhouse in a cool shaded position, and gradually expose to full light.

GREENHOUSE FLOWERS

Achimenes

Grown from small catkin-like tubers. Many named cultivars in rich colours. Often grown in hanging containers. Start into growth late winter/early spring in a propagator at 18°C (64°F), with 6–7 in each pot. They like moderate humidity, warmth, and shade in summer.

Azalea

Dwarf named varieties of hardy evergreen azalea are sold by many garden centres. But those bought in flower at Christmas time are varities of deciduous *Rhododendron simsii*. Stand them outdoors in summer, returning to a warm greenhouse in autumn. Always keep azaleas moist with lime-free water.

Begonias

There are many lovely types including a range of exotic foliage kinds. Grow the giant double-flowered exhibition types from tubers started in a propagator in early spring at 18°C (64°F). They will flower in 13cm (5in) pots. Single and multiflora begonias and pendulous varieties for hanging baskets can also be grown from tubers. Fibrous-rooted bedding kinds, from March-sown seeds, also make fine pot plants.

Browallia speciosa

Produce pretty blue or white cup-shaped flowers in winter. Sow seeds in late winter in a warm propagator to flower the next autumn onwards. Modern varieties like 'Troll' are less than 30cm (12in) tall. Older varieties may be double this, so pinch out tips of seedlings to encourage branching. Pot several seedlings in each pot.

Calceolaria

Brilliantly showy with masses of pouch-shaped inflated blooms in many bright colours. Sow in late spring to early summer. Grow them on in trays, later potting them individually in 10cm (4in) or larger pots, depending on the variety. Many are offered in flower from Christmas to late spring. Giant forms are usually late spring flowers. Winter minimum 5°C (41°F).

Varieties of *Rhododendron simsii* are the popular Christmas-flowering azaleas. With care these can be kept from year to year – a large plant will produce a mass of blooms.

This is one of the winter/spring flowering begonias – 'Gloire de Lorraine'; not difficult to grow in a moderately heated greenhouse or conservatory.

ABOVE LEFT There are lots of different forms of greenhouse chrysanthemums. This is one of the single-flowered varieties, excellent for cutting.

ABOVE RIGHT The cascade chrysanthemums are easy to grow and can be trained to various shapes but mostly they are encouraged to trail from staging.

Camellia

These glorious flowering evergreens make fine pot plants for an unheated greenhouse while they are young. They flower well and benefit from protection from extreme cold. Never let the pots dry out and always use lime-free water.

Campanula

C. pyramidalis, the chimney campanula, forms a column massed with cup-shaped blue or white flowers, about 1.3m (4½ft) tall. Sow in spring, overwinter in frost-free conditions, then move to large pots the next spring to flower in summer. *C. isophylla* also has blue or white flowers, but is a trailer. Kristal Hybrids, available from seedsmen, can be grown from seeds sown in a propagator in February.

Capsicums and solanums

Neat bushy plants with bright yellow, orange, or red berries – capsicum fruits are usually elongated, solanums (winter cherry) spherical. The latter is popular at Christmas time. Sow from February to April, solanums the earlier. Capsicums are quick to fruit, easier, and may be decorative for summer. Stand solanums outdoors when flowering, for insect pollination. Solanum berries may be poisonous to children.

Carnations

Perpetual-flowering (PF) varieties are grown for cut flowers almost the year round. Buy rooted cuttings of named cultivars from a specialist in early spring. There are many to choose from, including low growing forms. Pot on to 18cm (7in) pots for flowering, giving careful support. Remove all the tiny buds that form around the main leading bud, to obtain large 'florist's' blooms. Give good ventilation and plenty of light. A number of varieties can also be grown from seed – see seedmen's catalogues for full details.

Chrysanthemum

There are numerous forms of this glorious flower. To become familiar with them study a specialist grower's catalogue. This will also advise on the ways of growing the different types. Most can be bought as rooted cuttings in spring. The giant exhibition types are grown *outdoors* during the summer then brought into the greenhouse in autumn to flower. They can follow a tomato crop. Charm chrysanthemums make neat pot plants with mounds of small blooms. Some excellent varieties can also be grown from seed – consult seedmen's catalogues.

Clivia miniata

Impressive spring-flowering plant with strap-like foliage and huge clusters of orange trumpet flowers on stout stems. Best bought as a young plant. Needs 25cm (10in) pot for flowering. When pots become filled with large fleshy roots give liquid feeds. Must be kept frost free, ideally 5°C (41°F) minimum.

Cuphea ignea

The Mexican cigar plant is a neat bushy plant easily raised from March sown seed. Smothered from summer to autumn with a mass of deep red, black and white tipped, tubular flowers.

Cyclamen

Well known for its winter flowers and silver-variegated foliage. Best bought as young plants in spring, or as tubers to start into growth from mid to late summer. Can be grown from seed sown in autumn, but takes about 14 months to flower. There are many named cultivars. Likes slight shade and steady temperatures, about 10°C (50°F) ideal.

Exacum affine

Dainty little plant with many small blue or white flowers with golden anthers. Should have a pleasing scent, but some modern seed strains are scentless. Sow March for late summer to autumn flowers. Put several seedlings to each 10cm (4in) pot. Can also be flowered in winter in moderate warmth. Likes good humidity, warmth and shade.

LEFT The Sim varieties of perpetual-flowering carnation are highly recommended. This one is 'Dusty Sim'.

ABOVE *Clivia miniata* can be grown in a cool greenhouse and flowers in the spring; allow it to become pot-bound.

Freesia

Well-known cut flower in charming colours and sometimes sweetly scented. Can be grown from seed sown in January for summer flowers. Sow direct in the pots in which they are to flower. Best grown from corms of *named indoor (not outdoor)* cultivars, from a bulb specialist, potted in August. Set 5–7 corms in each 13cm (5in) pot. Double-flowered forms are available. Likes airy, bright, frost-free conditions.

Fuchsia

Highly popular. Can be grown as a bush, a standard, in hanging containers, or in fancy trained shapes. Vast number of named cultivars. Choose from specialist catalogue, and buy as rooted cuttings in early spring. By pinching the tips of growing shoots, plants can be made to branch and trained to any shape required. For a standard, leave the growing tip of a rooted cutting but remove all side shoots (though not leaves) from the stem as it grows. Pinch off the tip when the desired height is reached. Many shoots will then grow from near the top of the stem to form the flowering head. Then remove leaves from the supporting stem. Always support with a cane. Stop pinching out 8 weeks before you require a plant to flower.

Gerbera

These handsome daisy-like flowers in lovely colours are prized for cutting. Short-growing varieties for pots such as 'Happipot' can now be easily raised from seed to flower summer onwards. Sow in February in a warm propagator. Pot the seedlings on to 13cm (5in) pots.

LEFT The hibiscus is a shrub and therefore can be grown as a permanent pot plant. The exotic-looking flowers appear in summer.

BELOW LEFT One of the most popular greenhouse climbers is the wax flower of Hoya carnosa. It is almost hardy but keep it frost free.

Hibiscus
A number of different types can be grown in the greenhouse, some sold as house plants. The hybrid 'Southern Belle' is easy from seed, outstanding if not amazing, and great fun. It has flowers the size of dinner plates in white and shades of pink and carmine. Sow seeds in a warm propagator in March and pot on to 23cm (9in) pots. It reaches about 1.5m (5ft) tall and flowers summer to autumn.

Hippeastrum
Popularly but wrongly called amaryllis. The large bulbs produce strap-shaped foliage, which often follows the enormous trumpet flowers on stout stems. There is a range of pleasing colours. Best bought as named hybrids from bulb specialists, and potted in 18cm (7in) pot with the tip well above the compost in early spring. Summer to autumn flowering. Best not dried off in winter, but kept just 'ticking over' in slightly moist compost and a minimum of 7°C (45°F). If these conditions can be provided they will remain evergreen as in nature.

Hoya carnosa
A climber with evergreen foliage, variegated in some forms, and clusters of starry flowers, cream to dark pink sometimes fragrant, early summer to autumn on mature plants. Almost hardy, but best kept frost free. Water the plant well in summer but keep nearly dry in winter. Likes good light and moderate humidity during summer.

Gloxinia
Popular late summer to autumn-flowering plants with velvety foliage and clusters of huge showy trumpet blooms in striking colours. Start tubers of named cultivars in early spring in a warm propagator. Pot in 13cm (5in) pots. Likes moderate humidity, warmth and shade.

Heliotropium peruvianum
(Cherry pie) A neat shrubby plant with large flattish heads of dark blue or purplish flowers with a strong distinctive scent. Sow seeds in early March and pot on to 13cm (5in) pots for summer to autumn flowering. 'Marine' is a recommended and popular variety.

RIGHT The sweetly scented late-flowering *Jasminum polyanthum* is a vigorous climber but can be restrained by pruning.

BELOW This is one of the New Guinea impatiens which have highly colourful foliage as well as being free-flowering.

Impatiens
The well-known busy lizzie. Many superb, quick flowering, seed strains are described in seed catalogues. Wide range of rich colours. Double forms have recently appeared. Sow in a warm propagator in March, then pot on to 13cm (5in) pots. Modern varieties do well in partial shade or even in direct sunlight outdoors so they can be used in bedding schemes.

Ipomoea
The morning glory is a favourite annual climber with large flowers like convolvulus. The variety 'Heavenly Blue' is still one of the best. Sow seeds in a warm propagator in early spring. Set three plants in a 25cm (10in) pot and provide something for them to climb. Give them a bright position and they will flower from summer to autumn.

Jasminum polyanthum
A very vigorous climber with strongly sweet scented tubular white flowers in profusion in late winter. Restrict plants to 25cm (10in) pots and provide support. Need a winter minimum of 4–7°C (40–45°F). Control growth simply by cutting back when necessary.

Kalanchoe
This succulent plant forms flattish red, pink, yellow or white flower heads from modern seed strains. Most are dwarf, making neat pot plants. Sow in a warm propagator in spring and you will have flowers the following winter to spring.

Lachenalia

L. bulbifera, often listed as *L. pendula*, is a small bluebell-like bulb with red, yellow, and purple tubular flowers, and pendulous habit. It is best displayed in a hanging basket by planting the bulbs through the moss lining 5-8cm (2–3in) apart. Plant in autumn for December flowering, place in a cool frost-free greenhouse not rising above 13°C (55°F). *L. aloides*, erect in habit, should be grown in pots, but in other respects is treated similarly.

Lilium

Many lilies can be grown in pots. The shorter growing kinds are the most suitable for a small greenhouse, such as the Mid-Century Hybrids and *Lilium speciosum* varieties. Pot in autumn and plunge as for spring-flowering bulbs. Always keep lilies cool. There are now many lovely hybrids so consult a specialist's catalogue when choosing. Most are delightful for an unheated greenhouse or conservatory.

Nerine

These large bulbs bear long stems carrying clusters of starry flowers in subtle shades of pink and red in autumn and early winter. For the greenhouse grow named hybrids of *N. sarniensis* from a bulb specialist, *not* the hardy outdoor forms, unless you want them for an unheated greenhouse. Pot in August with the tops of bulbs well above the compost. Moisten the compost and stand the pots outdoors in a cold frame. Give no more water until growth begins. Bring the plants into a frost-free greenhouse in autumn to flower.

ABOVE Lachenalias or Cape cowslips are grown from bulbs and generally flower during the winter. They thrive in a cool greenhouse.

LEFT Kalanchoes are neat dwarf succulent plants which flower over a long period. They can be raised from seeds.

Pelargonium

Usually, though incorrectly, known as 'geranium'. There are three main types for the greenhouse: the zonal or common geranium, the ivy-leaved of trailing habit suitable for hanging baskets, and the regal with short stemmed clusters of very large showy flowers. There are innumerable named cultivars of all kinds, obtainable as rooted cuttings from specialist nurseries in spring. All are delightful and no greenhouse is complete without some of them. Another group with scented foliage is also worth exploring.

It is also possible to raise splendid plants from F1 hybrid seeds. Sow these in February in a warm propagator and pot on to 13cm (5in) pots for summer flowering. These plants can be further propagated by taking cuttings. See seedsmen's catalogues.

Plumbago capensis

This is a wall shrub or climber with pretty phlox-like blue or white flowers from mid-spring to autumn. It can be bought as rooted cuttings or raised from seed sown in spring, when it will flower in its second or third year. Water well in summer, sparingly in winter and prune back after flowering. Winter minimum temperature should be 7°C (45°F).

ABOVE LEFT The ivy-leaved pelargonium is ideal for growing in hanging baskets. This is the variegated 'L'Elegante'.

ABOVE RIGHT An ideal wall shrub or climber for a cool conservatory – *Plumbago capensis*. It is long-flowering.

Primula and polyanthus

The three main primulas for greenhouse display are *P. sinensis*, (*P. praenitens*), *P. obconica*, and *P. malacoides*. They bear pretty flowers, the last-mentioned being particularly dainty. It forms a rosette of attractive foliage and stems of flowers borne in whorls. *P. kewensis* which, unlike the others has yellow flowers, is also sometimes grown. Sow in late spring to flower the following late winter to early spring. Winter minimum about 5°C 41°F).

Polyanthus and coloured primroses are splendid for an unheated greenhouse. Many varieties, including F1 hybrids, are described in the seed catalogues. Sow in late winter to early spring at not more than 16°C (61°F). Always keep them cool. All these primulas can be flowered in 10–13cm (4–5in) pots.

Salpiglossis

This half-hardy annual produces many richly coloured, exotically veined trumpet flowers. It is easy to grow from seed sown in March for summer flowering. Can also be sown in autumn and grown on over winter for spring flowering. Pinch the seedlings when they are a finger's length to promote branching growth. Recommended are 'Splash', an F1 mixture of colours, and 'Ingrid'.

Schizanthus

A half-hardy annual with masses of beautiful butterfly-like flowers in many colours and markings. Grow as described for salpiglossis. The newer dwarf varieties make splendid pot plants if several seedlings are set in each pot.

Streptocarpus

Forms many elongated trumpet flowers in various colours and long narrow spreading foliage. Named cultivars and hybrids can be bought as young plants. Can also be grown from seed sown in early spring to flower in autumn. Propagate after this by division. Likes moderate humidity, warmth, and shade. Give 13cm (5in) pots. Recommended from seed: F1 Concord.

Thunbergia alata

(Black-eyed Susan) Moderate growing annual climber with black-eyed rich orange flowers, but cream and white are available sometimes without the contrasting eye. Easy from seed sown in spring. Flowers from summer to autumn. Provide canes for climbing.

Foliage plants

These provide variety and make a background for flowering plants. Avoid any that need much warmth. The following can be recommended: aphelandra, foliage begonias, cissus, coleus (easy from seed), ferns, ficus, grevillea, jacaranda, marantas, peperomias, pileas, sansevierias and tradescantias.

TOP 'Splash' is a good variety of salpiglossis, a half-hardy annual easy to grow from seed.

CENTRE Schizanthus is another half-hardy annual very easily grown in cool conditions. This is the popular 'Hit Parade'.

BOTTOM Foliage plants for the warm conservatory include dracaenas, begonias and crotons.

FRUIT AND VEGETABLES

You can raise many plants for your vegetable plot in a greenhouse and get extra-early crops – particularly of tender plants that cannot be sown or planted outdoors until June. Sow them much earlier in a propagator and grow them on in pots. Harden them off before setting out. Examples are outdoor tomatoes, marrows, squashes, cucumbers, outdoor melons and sweet corn. Some hardier vegetables, like cabbages and cauliflowers also benefit from an early start under glass.

Some plants have become particular favourites for cropping under glass. Most greenhouse gardeners grow some of the following:

Tomatoes

(The most popular crop.) The sunny south side of a greenhouse is often devoted to them. They need moderate warmth so don't start too early or the cost of heating could make them unprofitable. Choose varieties from seed catalogues. There are large and small kinds, juicy and fleshy types, fancy shapes, yellow and striped ones. Moneymaker was once a great favourite but Alicante is now replacing it. Nurseries offer few varieties, but it is easy to raise your own from seed. Choose between Shirley, Odine (for small greenhouse), Mandel and Vibelco (good disease resistance), Supersonic (fleshy, good for sandwiches), Big Boy (huge fleshy fruits), Yellow Perfection (golden-yellow, fine flavour), Eurocross A (like Moneymaker but providing a more vigorous, better yield).

Sow as under Propagation from seed (page 21). Germinate best at 16°C (61°F). Sow late February to March in a frost-free greenhouse,

later for later crops. Prick out the seedlings in small pots and grow on until well rooted. Discard any weak, distorted, ferny, yellowish or mottled plants which could be infected with virus.

The simplest method is to plant three or four tomatoes in a growing bag. This gives excellent results with minimum fuss. Or you can use large pots of potting compost. You may get a good crop from planting in the ground the first year but crops later deteriorate. Many gardeners use ring culture, useful where the greenhouse is often unattended as it provides more constant moisture to

42

LEFT Tomatoes are the most popular of the summer crops. Grow on south side of greenhouse.

RIGHT Tomato 'Big Boy' has huge fleshy fruits with a very good flavour and excellent for slicing.

BELOW RIGHT To de-shoot tomatoes remove any shoots that grow on the main stems.

the roots. Grow the plants in potting compost in fibre cylinders (from garden shops) stood on a layer of shingle or coarse peat. The rings are liquid fed as required and the base aggregate is watered to keep it constantly moist. This method is suitable for automatic watering.

Tomatoes need secure support. Strong rough string is the simplest. De-shoot the plants by promptly removing shoots that grow in the angles between the leaves and main stem. Avoid wide fluctuations of temperature and moisture, which can cause flower and fruit drop, split skins and blossom end rot.

Special high potash feeds, such as ICI Liquid Tomato 'Plus', are available. Avoid temperatures over 27°C (81°F) and exposure to direct sunshine when fruits are ripening. Shade with white Coolglass. Fierce sun can cause green and yellow patches on the fruits and spoil them. Mist the flowers with water in warm bright conditions or gently shake the plants to help the fruits set.

Cucumbers

Next in popularity to tomatoes and well worth growing. A few plants can yield plenty of fine crisp flavoursome fruits. Cucumbers used to be

43

difficult to grow with tomatoes, as they needed more warmth and humidity. But the newer varieties are easy to grow and they can be safely treated with suitable modern pesticides.

Raise plants from seed, choosing 'all-female' varieties from the catalogues. You must pick male flowers off other varieties so the female flowers are not pollinated. (The males have no tiny fruit behind.) Pollinated fruits go to seed and become club-shaped and bitter. Set seeds on edge in the compost. They germinate easily at 18°C (64°F). Pot on as described for tomatoes. The easiest way to grow them is two to a growing bag.

Some of the new varieties give a useful crop if grown up a cane without any attempt to train them, but you then get a lot of fruits at first and few later. It is better to grow them on the staging and train them up strings or canes to the eaves. Remove all side shoots. Then train the stem over strings 15–20cm (6–8in) apart run across the roof. Tie the side shoots that form to these strings and stop the main stem when it reaches the topmost string. As fruits form, pinch out the tip of the lateral two leaves beyond the fruit. Secondary laterals should be treated similarly.

The plants crop for a long time, provided they are well fed (use a feed such as ICI Liquid Growmore) and watered. Never overwater cucumbers or the fruits will shrivel and turn brown while immature and the foliage will become sickly.

Lettuces

These are often grown in a greenhouse but are better in frames. If grown in the ground soil under glass they are likely to suffer from botrytis (grey mould). But they do well in

TOP Cucumbers used to be difficult to grow with tomatoes, but not so with many modern varieties.

ABOVE Lettuces make a useful winter crop in cold or cool greenhouses. Choose suitable varieties.

troughs made by lining trenches with polythene sheet slit to allow for drainage and filled with good potting compost. (Any suitable containers will do.)

Note that *not all lettuces are suitable for growing in greenhouses.* Seed catalogues state clearly which are. Sow the seeds and treat like bedding plants – grow on seedlings to a manageable size in seed trays before planting out where they are to crop. Be sure to give them good light and ventilation.

Sweet peppers

These have now become common-place in our kitchens but are not cheap to buy. You can grow your own easily, starting them as for tomatoes. A growing bag takes four plants. Several varieties are described in seed catalogues. They need little attention after planting apart from watering to keep their roots moist and feeding when the fruits are forming. Use a tomato feed such as Liquid Tomato 'Plus'. You'll need to thin the fruits of some varieties so each has room to swell properly. Late fruits can usually be ripened to yellow or red if picked and stored in a warm place indoors.

Aubergines

Can be grown in the same way as sweet peppers, but the plants grow tall – up to 1m (3½ft), so they need strong supporting canes. Fruits must be drastically thinned to leave three or four per plant. There are several varieties, the F1 hybrids being the best of the lot.

ABOVE Aubergines are as easy to grow as tomatoes but unlike that crop, the fruits must be drastically thinned out.

ABOVE LEFT 'Hot Gold Spike' is one of the hot peppers, generally used in oriental cookery.

LEFT 'Gypsy' is one of the many varieties of sweet peppers, which are no more difficult to grow than tomatoes.

Melons

The best greenhouse melons are the large Casabas. The small Cantaloupes are more suitable for frames. Grow melons like cucumbers, but space the training strings 25–30cm (10–12in) apart and the female flowers (with tiny melons behind) *must be pollinated*. Pick off a male flower and dust its pollen on the female flowers – pollinate them all at one go. The tiny melon behind each female flower should soon swell, showing it has been successfully pollinated. A few varieties are listed in seed catalogues. Hero of Lockinge does well in cool conditions.

Melons like plenty of light so it is not usually necessary to shade the greenhouse. When the fruits reach full size, reduce watering and give more ventilation. They are ripe when the end opposite the stalk feels soft when pressed gently with your finger and emits a fruity scent. Large fruits can be supported with nets improvised from mesh shopping bags or vegetable packs.

Grapes

A grapevine can demand the whole of a small greenhouse and prove a difficult companion for other plants. So it is a good idea to grow a few vines in pots instead. Suitable varieties are Royal Muscadine and Black Hamburgh. Pot them in 30cm (12in) pots in late December and plunge them outdoors until late winter. Give each pot two 1.5m (5ft) canes and tie a short cane between them at the top to form a loop. Take into the greenhouse and give a temperature of 10–13°C (50–55°F).

Suitable varieties of melon can be grown as a ground crop rather than as climbers like cucumbers. All, though, are suitable for cultivation in growing bags. Here the fruits are kept out of contact with the soil by means of plastic plant pots.

46

LEFT Grape vines take up a lot of space in a greenhouse when grown in the traditional way. This system might be better for a large conservatory.

BELOW 'Black Hamburgh' is the most popular of the black grapes and is ideal for growing in pots.

Train the vine up one cane and down the other. Lateral shoots will form and must be thinned to about 30cm (1ft) apart around the loop. As a bunch of grapes develops on each lateral, the shoot should be stopped two leaves beyond the bunch. The next winter, while the vine is dormant, remove half the cane that has formed and shorten the laterals to two buds. Vines grown like this must be discarded after three years and a fresh start made. But lateral shoots removed when pruning can be used as cuttings to propagate new plants as they are needed.

Strawberries

These are really a frame crop but a few pots could be grown in a greenhouse. Buy fresh plants each year and grow them on outdoors for a few months before moving them into 13cm (5in) pots or strawberry urns. They need a minimum temperature of 7°C (45°F). Pollinate by brushing fluffed-up cotton wool gently over the flowers. Watch for first signs of botrytis (grey mould) which is the worst enemy of this soft fruit.

Climbing French beans

These are a useful crop to precede tomatoes, provided you can maintain an average of 13°C (55°F). Germinate the seeds as for cucumber and transplant well-rooted seedlings to growing bags laid on the floor in a bright position. Train the plants up strings and stop each lateral at the third joint. Harvest beans as soon as ready or they could get tough. Selka, with stringless pods is particularly recommended for the greenhouse.

INDEX AND ACKNOWLEDGEMENTS

Picture credits

Pat Brindley: 1, 12, 20, 32(t), 36(tl), 38, 40(r), 41(c), 45(tr).
Ron & Christine Foord: 28(l).
John Glover: 8, 10(t), 18, 32(b), 33(t).
Derek Gould: 4/5, 25(t, b), 33(b).
ICI: 26.
S & O Mathews: 7(t), 21(r), 34(l, r).
Ministry of Agriculture, Fisheries & Food: 27(b), 28(r), 29(r).
Harry Smith Horticultural Photographic Collection: 6, 7(b), 9(t, b), 11, 15, 16(t, b), 21(l), 30/1, 35(l, r), 36(tr, b), 37(t, b), 41(t, b), 42, 43, 44(t), 45(t, b), 46, 47(t, b).
Michael Warren: 14, 24, 39(t, b), 40(l), 44(b).

Artwork by Simon Roulstone